THE CHOREOGRAPHER

The Choreographer

Prose Poems by
Gerald Fleming

SIXTEEN RIVERS
PRESS

Published by Sixteen Rivers Press
P.O. Box 640663
San Francisco, CA 94164-0063
www.sixteenrivers.org

Sixteen Rivers Press gratefully acknowledges the
National Endowment for the Arts for their support.

ART WORKS.
arts.gov

Library of Congress Control Number: 2012914846
ISBN: 978-0-9819816-7-3

Cover and interior design by Josef Beery

Cover photograph:
"Ballet master at the Opera de Paris watching a rehearsal"
by Alfred Eisenstaedt (Time and Life Pictures/Getty Images)

Author photograph by Jessica Linscott

Acknowledgments

Grateful acknowledgment is made to the editors of the following magazines, in which the following pieces, sometimes in slightly different form, appeared:

4'33" (U.K.): "The Choreographer"

Ambush Review: "Applause"

California Quarterly: "The Tones of Koto"

Forward to Velma: "Letter"

Hanging Loose: "Companionship," "No Man's Land," "The Subject," "The Traveler"

Litro (U.K.) and *The Packinghouse Review* (U.S.A.): "An Honest Cup of Coffee," "On a Tuesday, Not Writing"

Pearl: "Pasencore"

Prime Number: "Crucifixion, Kinetic"

PRISM International (Canada): "Man of New Skin"

The Same: "Gesture"

Snail Mail Review: "The Extraordinary Accordionist"

Versal (Netherlands): "Audio Guide: The Paintings You Missed"

Western Humanities Review: "Sephardic Airs: Variations"

Deep thanks to family members and friends who helped support this book in ways both literary and otherwise. Thanks to writers Ellery Akers, Bill Edmonson, and Judith Serin, whose eyes and ears inform each of these works. Thanks to the Sixteen Rivers Press team for their valuable and many-faceted support, to Skyler Fell, Anna Ling Kaye, Mia Johnson, Terence Winch, Keith Taylor, Jeffrey Greene, Joan Larkin, Robbie Long, Junji & Tomoko Yamashita, Heather Hartley, Vincenzo Giugliano, Elf Diggerman, Bob Hershon, Donna Brook, Marie Carter, Dick Lourie, Mark Pawlak, and Steve Gilmartin. Thanks to my kids, Gabriel and Jessica, to whom this book is dedicated and whose lives have helped make my own life the continuing joy that it is. And thanks as always to my wife Gerry, who continues to live with me, and for whose existence I'm immeasurably lucky.

for Gabe and Jess

CONTENTS

There have been men who have been more remembered than nations, and nations of men have been willing to die for a word.

Then my word or your word?

Don't be impudent, child.

—Elizabeth Smart
By Grand Central Station
I Sat Down and Wept

1

The Subject

SHE DIDN'T SEEM TO BE a talker, so as she set up the photograph he had time to sit in her faded canvas chair and think. He had a sense that she didn't want him to watch her—that the setup of the cameras, the lights, the white backdrop, though routine, had an obsessiveness that was private—so he turned his face away.

What a gift at my age, he thought, to be approached by a beautiful woman at the café where I misspend my mornings—to be drinking coffee, reading the paper, and for her to come and ask—and so directly!—*May I photograph you?*

Was it the beret he'd been wearing lately—not, he hoped, as an affectation, but because it was a warm hat that fit and looked decent—unlike those others that men wear, rising like miniature buildings from the body? He liked the beret: rain beaded and rolled off its black wool, and he could pull it so tight that the entire top of his head was warm.

Why do I tilt it, then, if warmth is all? Why black and not pale blue, why do I regard my gray hair as distinguished only when the beret's on? Deluding myself even now—what a pleasure it continues to be, he thought. And as to the artist-in-beret notion, he tried to turn his thoughts away from that, then remembered, dimly, a scene from long ago: an art studio, a dreary day in London's Mile End, a mound of white clay in front of him, a dazzling white model, a teacher shouting *Let's get going, people—use that clay!* And he, hunched there, para-lyzed—kneading and kneading the clay, nothing forming from his hands, and then the model's time was up and she was gone.

"Here?" he asked. "In this café?"

"No," she said. "In my studio." And he was a man, after all, she a lovely woman—tall, bent beside him now so that her gaze would equal his as she spoke. Her approach had made him feel virile, but her stance beside him then and the volume of her voice made him feel feeble, patronized. Still, the mystique of *studio, photograph,* had a suggestion that pleased him—did not *stir* him, but served to reprise a smug-ness he thought he'd conquered long ago. He realized now he'd never vanquish it, for in part it defined him: a smug-ness seen by others as arrogance but that in fact was study: study of others, yes, but equally of himself—and after many years of such attention, discerning patterns and enjoying their repetition with intense pleasure: it was as if the entire human world were performing only for him.

Now, in the canvas chair, he thought about a scene he'd witnessed earlier as he ordered his coffee. Two young men and a young woman working behind the counter: one man in steam at the handle of the espresso machine, the other at the cash register, the attractive young woman between.

"You're not feeling well, Michael—you should go home," she said to the man steaming milk, and came up behind him and put her hands on his chest and hugged him quickly, her head turned, her cheek on his back, and he said, "Oh, I'm okay—I'll stay..." and the young man at the register saying, "Andrea, you're nice—such a good buddy..." and the young woman straightening her body and, in feigned outrage, her hands held Italian, her accent now Italian, her voice deepening, saying, "*Buddy? Buddy?* I don't want to be *nobody's* buddy. I want to be *lovers*—" the *o* in *lovers* drawn out, Andrea disappearing into the back room, the two young men laughing, but each undone.

What power, the man in the beret thought. How little these young men know what just occurred—they sensed it, their legs perhaps weakened by her beauty and her words and the quick grace of her exit—but it was clear they did not understand fully. Certainly there was the erotic power of it—each would later think on that—but, larger, this assertion of biology rarely seen so patently. He was once a young man, too.

Pure *surge*, he thought. Morality? Ha! What does the body understand? The commandments of swell and spew, of *take in*, of skin on skin, twist and thrust. We're all under arrest.

But he was calm, self-possessed as he sat waiting in the photographer's studio—flattered that there was something in him that interested her. Did he dare ask?

He asked.

"I'm not sure," she said, as she set up a flat computer screen on the floor below the cameras. "Maybe some of the lines in your face." (*Some* of the lines? he thought.) "Maybe some *spark*." And she let it go at that.

I have *spark*, he thought. I'm the subject of a photography session. And he wondered what genre he belonged to: Man Ray, Dorothea Lange? Or maybe Arbus. He hoped it wasn't Arbus.

"I feel like a paramecium," he said to her, and it was clear that his sudden interruption disturbed her in her work, but then engaged her, for she stopped, turned toward him and smiled.

"You feel like a paramecium?"

"Yes—you're taking slides, aren't you? Paramecium 2523, Sedimentary Soil, Western San Francisco."

She laughed.

"Well, remember that paramecia have the ability to swim in reverse," she said. "Want to back out?"

He was delighted. What if she'd said, *Oh, don't be silly*, he thought, or said *That's cute*, or, worse, what if she just looked at him, dead-eyed, he the object, soon to be vitrified.

He didn't push it. "It's just these cilia," he said, and flicked back the stray hairs over his ears.

She took off her shoes—her toes long, the nails painted green—put on a pair of Chinese slippers, and said, "Let's begin."

On a Tuesday, Not Writing

IT'S ASTONISHING HOW much time you can sift away doing nothing. Just yesterday, from your place six thousand miles from home, you told two people on the phone that your writing was going nicely, that it took a week to get the ball bearings oiled, but now you're *on a roll*, and things are fine.

And things *were* fine, yesterday.

But today, you woke up feeling a little shitty yet not shitty enough to call yourself sick, and it's raining, and the calendar says it's mid-spring but you haven't seen the sun for ten days, and you realize that you *talked about it*, that the writing was going well and your first rule is *never* to talk about it when *anything's* going well because it might evaporate, it always does: the fuel pump goes out ten minutes after you've said *great car*, an incisor shatters the moment you finish bragging about not needing to give any damned dentist a cent of your hard-earned money, and the living/breathing topics of your writing dry up, dead seals on the beach. But it's okay—you forgive yourself—you'll get to it, and anyway the dishes need to be done—and then dried, of course, and you need to finish that article on Mailer's letters to Styron, and then you see another, an interview with this writer Kennedy who lives in Copenhagen, a guy you're sure you'd like if you met him, would drink a couple of beers with him in what he calls *serving houses*, and you think about Denmark, about drinking, remember the Danish man you met in Athens when you were traveling with your wife and kids, he said *Come visit if you get to Denmark*, and you did visit, and he took you to his woodshop and gave you a carpenter's plane, an antique, 1889, it said, and at dinner he got half-drunk but stayed gentle, but his wife didn't like his drunkenness so they got into an argument, shouting, the wife asking you *Don't you think I'm right?* and this wasn't Discourse: European we're talking about here, it was her complaining that every weekend he goes with his pals and they ride the ferry back and forth between Rødby and Puttgarden, all Saturday night into Sunday because they're in international waters and no state can shut down the bars as they do in their town and because the booze is cheaper, and he just keeps paying for more booze, more rides, and you and your wife wouldn't take sides and the woman turned angry at you for not doing so, she herself drunk now, *Don't you have an opinion*, she'd say, not interrogative but accusative, and you hardly knew these people, and you said *No, no opinion*, and *No thanks* to their offer of beds, you were all set up to sleep in your camper van, so you slept out in their driveway, the kids tired, quick to sleep, but your wife and you saying *What the hell was that about?* and laughing, and you got out of there as fast as you could the next day.

You're still reading the Kennedy article, killing time so you don't have to Face It, and you remember a cool thing the Dane showed you. You'd worked with wood quite a bit by that time, and remarked on the beautiful finish of their pine floors. *Ivory soap*, he said, and explained that you get a box of Ivory Flakes and slowly add water, make a paste, put it on with a cloth, buff it when it's dry, that's it. Easy to clean, and when it starts to wear, repeat.

Time's moving on, and this is great, because you'll have fewer hours to write. *This is terrible.*

So, check e-mail, and write a few, one telling Maria the editor that you misspelled S. K.'s name—here's the correct spelling and thanks, and sorry, and you think of the hero she is, she and Ricardo and Herb, putting out that magazine year after year, poor and staying poor, but true to The Word and to their word. There should be a prize, a Nobel category: Science, Literature, *and this year's winner, in the category of Tenacity…* —and you know that if she came into money she'd just keep doing the same thing, a magazine about poetry—who in this world can imagine such a thing? She can, they can, you think, and the raindrops on the metal ledge outside make you feel inundated, and you think about that, about—what was it, two summers ago?— Paris, *Piscine Pontoise*, that was the name of the swimming pool just a few blocks off the Seine... you wonder if it has a website, and sure enough, there it is—all art deco, blue water, two stories of blue-doored changing chambers, a roof that retracts on the dozen days a year Paris gets good weather—remember that they wouldn't let you wear your baggy American trunks, they gave you Speedos, and it was a damned good thing you knew no one. Still, it was fun, and that mini-park down from the pool—solitudinous enclave among stone buildings. You ate a sandwich there.

Time to get a sandwich at the bakery up the alley. The good ones will be gone if you don't go now. Chicken and sliced eggs and that homemade mayo. Out the door you go.

Back soon, but before eating let's clean this place up. Put away the dishes. Wipe the counters. And that stove top—when your wife gets here next week she will not be happy, and wouldn't it be passive aggressive just to let it go, have her do it out of her own you-call-it-compulsion-but-she-calls-it-simple-sanitation? Buff that baby up now—it'll just get worse—get it while it's easy.

The sandwich, delicious. You finish the Kennedy article (funny, just last night you read a *Ted* Kennedy article—Kennedy's father saying *There will be no crying in this house*, and another scene—very young Ted doing something silly, childlike, and his dad summoning him for a conference, saying *I love you and will continue to love you, but I am finding you not Serious, and if you continue to be not Serious, I will have no time for you. I have too many other children who have chosen to be Serious, and it is they I'll pay attention to . . .*

And of course you're horrified when you read that, but now wonder if you've led a Serious life, been Serious—or did you have too damned much fun, too much laughter, too little work?

The night before you were reading about Sam Johnson, a review of a new book about him, and the author talked of Johnson's prodigiousness—that dictionary! That Shakespeare! Two lives right there, but also, simultaneous, his own copious writings, and you liked how the author of the article marveled at today's writers, who complain *My novel's not coming together, I can't write more than two hundred words a day lately, the writer's life is so* hard . . . And then, of course, to remember that Johnson—and every other writer until recently—wrote each word by hand, and indeed even with the advent of the typewriter, every draft was *done again*—remember those days? Typing it again, again, and still making errors, sticking the skinny flat tapes in, backing up the carriage, then typing *not the correction* but *the same error* again so that the white paint on the back of the tape would enter that black "f" in *finger* and you'd go back again, type in the proper "l" for *linger?* Oh, boy.

And this pale labor you're involved with, anyway: have you emptied the well? It does give you comfort that on your way up the street for the sandwich you passed a tall young guy, black T-shirt, bread-loaf belly, gold earring, leaning against the building in the rain and making a phone call.

You wondered whom he was calling, and why out there in the rain, and that wonder itself gave you hope—you're still interested in the narrative, the great un-umbrellaed narrative.

So now you'd better get to work. There's a mockingbird singing, and its subject is you.

The Plowman

EVERYWHERE HE WALKED he felt he was pulling a plow. From the moment he arose, he felt pulled backward—always his forward motion impeded, as if he were harnessed, the moldboard behind him, the coulter and the share dragging aimlessly on the floor, into the street, across the field between his office building and the next, always the sense of reticence, but more than that.

As a boy, he felt he could never move quickly: running did not suit him—not once did he like it—and his first memories were of his father bellowing *Hurry up*, the big face turning flatly toward him, its cruel scowl.

He couldn't. He just couldn't. He wasn't fat, he wasn't weak, he simply felt . . . held back.

He feigned sickness in high school gym class, but the coach made him run laps anyway, and of course he finished last—the coach, scowling like his father, standing with his stopwatch, tapping it dramatically. These were the little embarrassments.

One summer, his parents took him to Southeast Asia, and on an early-morning bus ride in Cambodia, rounding a curve, he saw an ox in harness, the ox pulling a walking plow, a small man trudging behind, working the metal into the ground.

Later, on that same trip, when his parents urged him to hurry as they walked city streets and country lanes, the triangularity of that plow came into his mind—a recognition made more by his body than by any process of thought, where one idea leads to another. No, this was body to body, a reckoning of one's place on earth, one's *pace*. He was the ox.

As he grew, then, that Southeast Asian plow was always with him as he walked, and each month he brought forth—in his own mind, of course—more specifics of his encumbrance: the thick leather strap around his hips, the rusted metal of the frame, the decrepitude of the clevis, the powdery oxidation of the moldboard—all, it seemed, moving toward self-definition, acceptance. So as he moved into manhood it didn't bother him much that people would turn and look when they saw him hunched forward on the boulevard, plodding his way home.

But one thing did come to bother him: the sense of getting no purchase, no depth. If indeed he was pulling a plow, toward what purpose? A good walking plow needs to be guided, its draft animal goaded, chided, its steel shined by the soil it tills, furrow after furrow, day after day. And as these thoughts increased, his sense of sorrow and aimlessness did, too.

I need a partner, he thought. I have been put on this earth to be useful.

He advertised: knew he could not seek a plowmate, so advertised for *friendship, and, should it grow, affection.*

He met people at cafés. Men. Women. *Shall we take a walk down the street?* he'd say, and then, *Would you mind walking just behind me, and talking to me from there?*

Some excused themselves and left. Others tried it, some even calling out his name as they walked, and that made him very happy.

But finally, no one was adequate. Some walked behind for a while and he'd feel perfectly balanced, then they'd foolishly draw up beside him and begin chattering like crows, and once he lost his temper with a charming woman, shouting *Get back there! I told you!* and oh, she went back, all right: she turned and walked the other way.

The man's deepening understanding of his encumbrance, down now to the properties of iron and what the surface area he traversed might do to that iron, what every weather would do to his dried old strap and moldboard, his sense of the ground behind him fallow and unfurrowed led him not to despair but to resignation: this was his place in life.

No-Man's-Land

THE GUEST HAS DECIDED to stay. He's called our house his country, and though we never told him we didn't believe in countries he must have guessed it by the words we used—*jingoism, borderlessness*—what a mistake it was to drink wine with him, say what was on our minds.

He's planted a flag in the room we've let him sleep in. You went in to make his bed while he was out for a hike, and saw it there. The flag's on a little metal stand on the table beside the bed, pale blue, and your face is on it.

You came out and told me that. You were shaken, but not for the reasons I thought. You said it was the most beautiful photo of you you'd ever seen, it was as if he'd taken a picture of you on your bike as a child speeding down Chestnut Grade in summer—wind, you said, free, before you met me, you said, long before you met me, but this picture on the flag was of you as a woman, and you didn't understand.

Go look, you said.

I went to look. You'd put a lily on his pillow.

We can't ask him to leave now, you said, he's claimed his

territory, it doesn't seem unreasonable—the kids are gone, we hardly use that room, and he's charming, really, don't you think?

He took my walking stick, I said. The one I cut from the old madrone, the one I carved to fit my own hand, and now he's out in the hills with it.

I let him use it, you said. It rained so hard last night, and the trails are slick, and there's the creek he'll have to leap across.

You let him use my walking stick?

And he needed a hat, so I let him use your hat.

What else did you give him? I asked.

I gave him a bucket to gather chanterelles. He said he wanted to sauté chanterelles tonight; we'll eat the first ones fresh from the pan, and I told him fine, we'll have that Bordeaux we put away, but he said he'd better taste it first to see if it's right, it must be just right, and he liked it, and we both had a bit of it, and there's still a little left in the bottle, I think, you were at work or we would have given you some, but I didn't know then about the flag—the flag is beautiful, don't you think?

The flag is beautiful, I said.

So you can see why I left the lily?

I can see, I said.

And you'll come down to dinner, dear, won't you? We're having chanterelles, he's showing me how to recognize chanterelles. How wonderful just to say their name, isn't it?

Chanterelles, I said.

He's sweet about this flag thing, this country thing, you said. We were standing in the kitchen drinking wine, and he said to me I'll be the king and you'll be the queen, dilly dilly. Okay, I'll be the queen, I said, and he came over to me, he put his hands around my waist, like this, and he said the queen has her queenly duties—and I shouldn't have liked it, I suppose, but I said yes, the queen does have her queenly duties. And he said this was a no-man's-land before, wasn't it—and now I claim it. Do you think this was a no-man's-land, do you think so? And oh, he seemed a little anxious about the mountain lion on the ridge—someone saw it again last week—so I gave him your pistol, too.

The Tones of Koto

As a young man, he'd read *The Tale of Genji* many times, knew whole passages by heart, and was certain that one day he, too, would be passing through a town—maybe on his old home Hokkaido, maybe on Shikoku, and from an alley he'd hear the tones of koto, would follow the thin river of that sound—and there, at its source, on a bamboo mat behind the louvers of an open window, she would be.

He deferred love, then: let no one in. Went from island to island as a traveling salesman, wandered the streets of each town he came to, wore out many pairs of shoes. He aged: bending more by the year, balding, penurious, then one April evening in his sixty-fourth year, veered into a steep alley outside Takagama, imagining as always that he heard koto—*climbed* the sound, it seemed, up that alley, lost it—panicked a moment—found it again and followed, up, up, around a bend to another alley where the paving stones lay upheaved by the ice of many winters, and when he drew closer to the source—those same stones now carpeted with cherry blossoms so thick they silenced his feet—he saw her there: on a soiled tatami mat behind a broken louvered window, the crone contorted over her koto, each of its thirteen thick strings broken except one, and that one string, itself obscured in a profusion of white hair, that one string plucked over, over, violent, bitter, profane, notes going nowhere except into their duplicate, the rote vocabulary of her years.

We want him to interrupt her. We want him to stand tall, call out, announce himself in the old way, say *At last I've found you*, and we want her to draw up her own bent spine, twist her hair deftly into a bun, to restring, change her tune, play "Hachidan" inimitably, rise from the bamboo, and yes, we admit it—we want them to sweep away years like cherry blossoms, like koto notes, her breasts to rise, her hair go crow-black, we want in him the old radiance we saw when we first knew him, who held the *Genji* in his hand and hewed to his vision before he weakened and went lost, before he turned away on those same paving stones, before we watched him in his clipped-stepped flight down the darkening alley, toward Takagama again.

Applause

FOR EXAMPLE, you're in a strange city—*this* strange city—it's night, and you go into a café—any café with good reading light—and the waiter seats you at a table against a bare white wall, and the guitarist, whom you did not notice—short beard, kind eyes—begins playing, and before even opening your book—say, Calvino's *If on a Winter's Night a Traveler*—you're moved by the guitarist's rendition of a difficult Spanish song, and you decide at the end to applaud, and find in that full café yours is the only applause.

It's not that you're embarrassed, but worried that you've embarrassed *him*, and though he smiles and nods to you in a dignified way, you feel that in the loneliness of your applause you've brought attention to the fact that he, though a true artist, supplies no more than background music here, and you imagine that you've perhaps served to deepen the depressive state he's been in for weeks, this appearance tonight his one great effort to overcome paralyzing inertia, to keep his promise to himself, to move into the world.

You've had a hard time reading in the apartment you've rented—the dog with the high-pitched bark across from you relentless, the kids downstairs incessantly fighting, so you withdraw here, pick up your book, again find the middle of Calvino's Chapter Eight, try respectfully to split your attention between the narrator's walk with the Okeda family beside the lake and the guitarist, who has begun another song, but whose virtuosity, already idealized by you, diminishes when you discover that the song is a cheap tune from a Broadway musical—no more than a series of chords, really.

You're torn, for your intention tonight was *attention*— good light for the Calvino, steady progress in its coiling narrative, a time for your body to be sipping coffee in a café in a strange city while your mind is in a different place— two places at once, really—in Rome, where you imagine Calvino writing at a mahogany desk in a second-story room overlooking Piazza Navona, and in rural Japan, where the narrator, on his stroll by the lake with the Okedas, pauses, kneels on a rock, leans toward the water, and in reaching for water lilies, assisted by Makiko, Mr. Okeda's daughter, and Madame Miyagi, Mr. Okeda's wife, feels the sudden touch of Makiko's breast at his right arm, Madame Miyagi's at his left.

The song is coming to an end, and you're torn: do you applaud again, thus not only insuring your continued lonely tribute after each number, enslaving yourself to it, and binding yourself, too, to the guitarist, who perhaps will wish you'd never applauded in the first place (his vortex of depression spinning even faster), but also compromising yourself by applauding a poorly chosen song, thus emboldening the guitarist to search his sheet music for more chordal horrors, insuring your early departure, progress in the Calvino impeded once again?

The song ends, and you put down the book and applaud—the man is working, this is his art, for that he deserves praise—he's more respectable than you, really, for he's *practicing* his art while you, who call yourself a writer, have escaped to a café in a distant city where instead of working you seek a corner to read a foreign book, the sinuousness of that book reflecting, perhaps—how are you to know?—the ambivalence in the guitarist's mind as he hears the first report of that applause: this time, though, not solitary, you're relieved to discover, but joined by four others at the table nearest him—four who now, though present earlier for the accomplished Andalusian fretwork, feel roused to applaud this tawdry Broadway tune.

You look at them: the five of you imprisoned now, and you know it, but at least, you think, as the guitarist begins again and the foursome in your book returns to the Okeda house, at least you have company—good people, whose musical tastes, though different from your own, are to be respected—and you hope that their kindness might spread from table to table, and that soon, as the entire café is committed to applause, the guitarist will not miss yours, and you will be able to sink again into your book to discover whether the narrator, now back in that tranquil Japanese home—Mr. Okeda safely in his study—will entangle himself with the body of Mr. Okeda's daughter, or that of Mr. Okeda's wife.

But at the end of this song—not bad, the guitarist having changed his acoustic guitar for an electric in order to achieve the steel tones of rock and roll, *soft rock*—you find to your dismay that your four compatriots—who already you've felt were family—have gone silent again, yours the only hands heard.

You wish you'd never come into the café, and recall your wife chiding you about your *compulsion*, she called it, to be demonstrative, this by-product of what seems to her an innate extroversion—and you know that she's correct, but your ambivalence, like that of the kind-eyed guitarist, begins to swirl about you, for your introverted side yearns only for quiet, especially just now, when the narrator, having made an inappropriate comment arousing Mr. Okeda's daughter, enters the room where Mr. Okeda's wife is kneeling, arranging flowers.

You can't stay: call for the check, see that there's a fee for the music, a quiet night in a café now degenerated into a costly enterprise where a cup of coffee was only one-fifth the price of applauding three times for half an hour of acoustic confusion, the book and its unfinished chapter in your right hand, the café bill in your left, the under-kimono areola of Mr. Okeda's wife in the narrator's hand.

You walk home, the streets empty after rain, wondering what your intention was tonight after all, whether you did the right thing in choosing to give your attention to a man playing guitar in an obscure café in a strange city, and giving Calvino—love him as you do—only part of you, his book in your satchel, and you find yourself looking at your hands now as you walk under a halogen streetlight, remembering that you tried to catch the guitarist's eye as you left, to wave goodnight, but he was playing.

Letter

January 14, 1910

Dear Marie,

I received your letter yesterday, and, like you, I <u>do</u> wish you had more time to write. Each of your words is precious to me, and as I read them again and again they take on a rather magnified importance, I fear—an importance unfair to you.

I suppose I can say things are fine here, but the winter already is wearying, and though I am not an old man, today the prospect of repeating winter after winter does not appeal.

Luck is with me, certainly. The roof patch I did in November has held, and the whole place is dry, even in our January deluge. And the firewood dry, and the kindling— thank God for that. Lamp oil low, but Jansen's has plenty this year.

The nights, though, Marie, are long. One <u>knows</u> that, of course, it's the cycle, but knowing it and living it have somehow become more difficult for me in the years you've been gone. A gap is there, and not simply because you are not by my side. It is as if my body itself does not understand what has happened as fall moves into winter. When winter arrives, my body is always surprised.

At the equator it must be so hard for you to remember that dark comes early here these months. At around 3:30 I make my rounds, checking that the candles are in their proper places, that the log crib is filled, the kindling restocked, the lamp-wells high, the wicks good.

And every night the word <u>Electrification</u> sings in my ears. Over the hill they have a whole different life, Marie. They read by glass filaments at midnight!

I <u>have</u> been reading, though. Dark falls fully by four, I get my evening going—the stove and the lamps and candles—putter around making dinner, have my beer, and settle in. I'm reading <u>The Little Courtesy Book</u> by Mason and Fowles. Why, I don't quite know, but I <u>am</u> being instructed. For example, upon leaving special events, one should never "rush around fawning farewells to each and every one, unless the gathering is very small." And, at a dinner party, if I should drop a piece of silverware onto my lap, I am to ignore it "until a servant comes into the room, then tell him in quiet tones."

So you see, Marie, I will be quite the proper gentleman when you return.

Mother is not doing well. It's the hip again. I won't go into details just now, but I do visit often. If I miss a visit, Mother certainly lets me know.

Marie, that photograph you sent—I cannot tell you how

much I enjoy it. Imagining from here the ability to open to the warm air so much skin! Your face is so dark, Marie—and that blouse—is it native?

I have made it a practice not to be a jealous man. I am good at it, after this long. But not perfect. That gentleman you're with, Marie, in the picture, the one in the straw hat and smoking the cigarette: is he a fellow scientist? The two of you look so happy, as if you had discovered a new species. A smile like that on your face can fuel my days, Marie.

Well, my Courtesy Book tells me that when one says "Good-bye," one ought to do so quietly and not prolong it. The wind is coming up, those clumps of cedar you like for their fragrance are being blown from the trees, and I'd better get more wood in. So farewell for today, Marie, and though I'll have written you many times over before your next precious post arrives in my box (how <u>many</u> of your letters must have been lost! I admit I sometimes curse the word <u>Sumatera</u>), when it arrives, it will be as if the first.

In great fondness, as always,

Walter

The Traveler

WAKES IN THE MIDDLE of the night in Hama, Syria. He has a tremendous pain in his liver, and is certain he can know the length of his liver by the length of his pain. He and his wife had dinner at their hotel that evening: a good deal, a meal served at a common table with three traveling Germans, the main course a delicacy: Iraqi truffles served with beef and seasoned rice.

This was the most delicious meal we've had in all of Syria, the traveler said to the owner on the way back to the room. They shook hands.

Now, in the dark of night, a desert wind blasting through gaps in the black window, shaking its frame, the traveler considers the wide web of trust that binds together the living—every other breath, it seems, a contract.

He knows it was the truffles, thinks perhaps they were mushrooms, thinks of newspaper stories he's read at home: naïve fungus hunters trooping into hills, digging, filling their pails, coming home, having a glass of wine, cooking, the mushrooms delicious—then, hours later, pain, liver failure, death.

What are the chances of getting a liver transplant in Syria? Or the chances of *two* liver transplants, one for his wife, too, sleeping so soundly beside him, the sound of her breath the rhythmic tick of a time bomb?

The traveler is thirsty. A classic symptom, he thinks.

Should he call the embassy in Damascus before he loses consciousness? Should he alert the Germans in the room next door—one of whom spoke good English and at dinner announced she *didn't like stone*, and wondered aloud why she came to Syria—especially as a tour guide?

This could be nothing, the traveler thinks, but it's not nothing: he knows it. And liver failure? Inevitable in the time it'd take them to be medivacked to London.

He turns in his hard bed, decides to accept his fate. He gets up, pulls a piece of paper from his notebook, finds his pen, goes into the bathroom, switches on the light, shuts the door so as not to disturb his dying wife, closes the toilet lid, sits on that weak plastic, and begins to work:

"Let it be known that I, traveler, on this 23rd day of March, did, at the Hotel Noira in Hama, Syria, ingest, along with my dear wife, a meal said to contain truffles, which I am now certain were poisonous mushrooms.

"Let it be known further that this traveler, whose gentle wife still sleeps, awaiting her certain doom, is resigned to his fate, but does not die without regrets.

"Let it be said in ceremonies that this traveler did indeed die doing what he enjoys: traveling. But let it also be said that he regrets convincing his wife to come with him from Turkey to Syria, extolling Palmyra and Afamia, exploiting her love of antiquities, delivering the coup de grace with a rendering of the life of the magnificent Queen Zenobia. Let it be said that this traveler died in a mire of ulterior motives, and that ultimately he did not fail to see the irony that those same motives deprived him of his life.

"Finally, let it be told that the traveler would have preferred a quiet death in his own bed in his insect-eaten wooden house on the western edge of the North American continent, his right hand in his daughter's warm hands, his left in his son's, and his wife, sad and strong, stroking his head.

"Let it be known that the traveler's last act on earth was searching a phrase book, in vain, for what he wanted—something to summarize a life—but found only *We have missed our stop. Can you let us off here? When will a bus going the other way arrive?*

Remembering the Observatory

WE CLIMBED THE HILLS to the old observatory outside of town. No one in the town seemed to know exactly where it was, and the map you found in the village archives—faded, brittle, yellow at the edges—treated it as a footnote: small print, a little x beside what seemed to be a question mark, no elevation, no scale. So we walked maybe six miles, two brothers on a quest, all the while considering turning back, each prodded on by two citations in our great-grandmother's flighty, unrestrained poems, naming only "The Old Observatory" in one, "The White Observatory" in the other.

It would be on a hill, of course, but this was a land of hills. And I can't finally say what brought us, tired, wet with sweat, to climb that particular hill. We simply veered from the path and ascended.

There, hidden in a clearing inside a ring of blackberry brambles—curiously not at the apex of the hill but below it, facing a wide plain—it stood: a great octagonal dome of dark wood once windowed, most of its glass now gone.

We entered from under the building—no recent evidence

of humans, no garbage, no piss smell or condoms—stepped onto a stone floor, saw, at one end of the room, a serpentine staircase of tan stone. Four smaller rooms were on this level—two opposing two—mere cubicles, really, doorless, walled with the same tan stone, benches of stone inside each, and above each bench, iron hooks pounded into the gaps, as if places to hang clothes. Just outside these rooms, centered under the great room above, a circle of sunken stone, as if a disused pond or a tub for bathing or a shallow cistern. *Strange*, we said, and started up the stairs.

Ascending into the observatory itself made us think of a time when we were much younger, when on a trip with our wives, half-drunk with red wine, we climbed the steps of Sainte-Chapelle—bursting, it seemed, into the resplendence of its stained glass. You touched my shoulder then, and touched it this time, too. Here was a wonder, to be sure, but not the same: there was glass all over the wooden floor, and what we saw when we looked up was no explosion of color, just the sky itself, framed again and again in the empty windows of the octagonal dome, in jagged panes of broken glass.

It was difficult to move around. Glass snapped everywhere we stepped, the floor layered with it. Decades of rain, the wood softening underneath, small patches of rot we tested, stepped away from.

How had so much wood stayed intact for so many years? You decided it had been treated—it seemed charcoaled somehow, evenly, intentionally. Even the mullions high above us, black.

And where was the place for the telescope, however simple telescopes were in those days? Surely it would have been in the middle, but though there was a second octagonal dome at the peak of the larger dome, we could see that in the center of the great room—whose tranquility we were only now beginning to feel—there was no railing such as we'd seen, say, at Greenwich, nor were there stanchions suggesting that either railings or any instrument had ever been bolted to the floor.

I walked around the room slowly—unable not to break more glass.

"Maybe they just sat here in chairs and looked at the stars," I said. "Or maybe they brought a bottle of wine, stripped off their clothes downstairs, came up, lay back in the summer heat, and just enjoyed the sky. I mean, there's no record of any *discoveries* here—it could have been built as a diversion— some rich man and his friends."

You shot me a look as if I had profaned the place. There was a grandeur there. I recognized my own shallowness, at least, and heard it again when I heard myself tell you I had to piss, thinking that would be a good excuse for us to leave; it was getting late, and I hated walking in the dark.

Recalling it now, it was only I who moved then, crunching glass. You stood transfixed, taller than I ever remembered you, your head turning. I can still see you there, standing.

"Wait," you said. "Look at those." Mounted high on the walls, beyond our reach and spaced apart evenly, four stone boxes: each of the same size, open semicircles behind a crude wooden perch at the front.

We looked at them, shook our heads.

"And look at this," you said, and bent and picked up a piece of dirty glass.

"Yeah. Broken glass," I said.

"No," you said. "Look. Really *look*."

I took it from you: held it to the light. Yes, broken glass. "Look!" you said, and I was relieved that you laughed, and realized for the first time that I was a little afraid of you.

I held it up. Its opacity seemed metallic, and in looking closer I saw a crazed tincture—perhaps silver—spat on it, rubbed off the spit with my sleeve, saw that it was mirror.

"They put up mirrors," you said. "The whole dome was mirrors—just look at the glass on the floor."

There was so much glass, the floor slick with it. I bent, examined, examined more: all mirror.

Then under the layers of fallen glass I saw a low spot, and bent there. It was floor, but it was not floor.

"Look here," I said. "They'd inlaid the floor with mirror. And look at this…"

I stepped toward you and held out a shard splashed with candle wax.

"My God," you said, and in retrospect it might have been close to something sacred. Who were these people, we wondered as we walked, the sky already dark, but the path known.

Did we stop talking even once, as we walked? About the strange men, and perhaps women—four of them, we figured, because of the four cubicles at the foot of the stairs—who built this place, brought in mirrors in a time when mirrors were made by hand, had them cut to fit, laid them in the floor, set them in the dome all around, left the upper dome empty—mullioned, but empty, and went there when: Sundays? Summer dusks? Solstices, equinoxes? Lit candles, took off their clothes in the stone rooms below, bathed, mounted the stairs, each candle refracted a thousand times in the octagon, then lay back on that mirrored floor, themselves silent, themselves refracted like those candles, and waited, watching the sky?

2

Sephardic Airs: Variations

In 2003, composer Jorge Liderman chose forty-six songs from Isaac Levy's Chants Judéo-Espagnols—*an anthology of fifteenth-century Sephardim music—and composed instrumental variations on each* (Aires de Sefarad, Albany Records, *2006). Though lyrics to the songs exist in Ladino, the following prose poems were based on the titles only, and adhere to Liderman's chosen order.*

POR LA TU PUERTA YO PASI

I come through your door, señora, and deliver your eggs. Your house so large, so fine, but I do not envy you. Our house is dark stone, our windows not windows but open spaces, and all day the wind persists. We like it like this. From one window we see the bay and the inn on the bay with its hanging lanterns. I will eat in that inn one day. Perhaps I will see you there, my dress as fine as the one you wear today.

ALCI MIS OJOS AL CIELO

I raised my eyes to the sky and I saw the sea. Mother—how can it be that such a dry place is so near the sea? Look up, Mother—are those not waves up there? We can call it down all we want, Mother says, we can say the clouds are gray waves, but these waves are bound for another place, meant for someone else. We'll have no rain today. But rain will come.

CINCO AÑOS YA VA A HAZER

It has been five years already since Nani left for Marseille. *Pretty doll*, my friend Silvana's father called her, but Nani was no doll. Nani, sister, when will you return? Last night I missed you more than ever. I slept, and all night the roads rose, fell, and it was cold, and I had no money, and I didn't know my way to Marseille.

MORENA ME LLAMAN

They call me Morena, my black hair I take from the raven, my black lashes from the crow, my skin from the ground we walk on. *Morena*, the lazy men say in their lazy way. I do not turn my head to look. It is water I come for, water I want. But they persist, like that wind they persist. How is it I enjoy it—being called something other than my name?

SE PASEAVA SILVANA

Silvana went for a walk and I joined her. We went far into the hills. What do you know of snow? she asked. Nothing, I told her. But I hear that there are mountains far from here where snow is on every road you walk, and in order to get into your house you must push it away from your door.

No, said Silvana, that cannot be.

Oh, I have heard other things, too, I said. I have heard that in places like that it is so cold that when you speak, your words rise in the air and can be seen.

No, said Silvana, and after that on our walk Silvana hardly spoke. When she did, she watched the air.

MI PADRE ERA DE FRANCIA

My father was from France, Mother told me once. Marseille is in France. Nani is in Marseille. I know that these three are things not together, but on a piece of paper I draw each of them as flowers—one blue, one red, one yellow. I cut them out and arrange them on the table. Each day I arrange them in a different way on the table, understanding that they are different flowers.

LA SOLEDAD DE LA NOCHADA

The solitude of the night sometimes frightens me. I can hear voices in the harbor, laughter, singing in the village, the great ships' horns. These for me are a kind of silence outside of silence, a want outside of want.

Pretty doll, Silvana's parrot says when anyone passes. Sometimes, these nights, I can't get that parrot's voice out of my mind, but it's not the parrot's picture I see—it's a doll made of lemonwood, a white girl, naked, breasts without nipples, staring into the sky. The rains will soon be here, Mother says. She says she can feel it on her skin.

But that other want I feel—it is not like wanting water.

LA MUJER, LA MI MUJER

That woman, my woman, I heard a man in town say today, dirt on his forehead, dirt on his chin. I could tell that he was not a thankful man. All of him was dirty—his hands dirty, too.

UN LUNES POR LA MAÑANA

On a Monday morning two weeks ago the old woman up the hill died. She had been bent over her work at a table in the shade in front of her house, her white hair all wild, her fingers like the vines of grape, the lines in her face a bird's nest. I saw her after she had fallen. It was not sad at all. I knew her, and for years she had been preparing. I didn't say it, but I had a thought that they should have left her there. It did not seem right when they picked her up.

NANI, NANI

Nani, Nani, you would not know me now. I have grown, Nani, I am taller, and dark hair appears in the most surprising places. When you left, even the old men grieved. You said they'd maybe miss the way you moved your hips, but that was all. You served me rose-petal tea the day you left. It made me dizzy.

Nani, remember that red skirt you had? The one with the straight-down white stripes next to the red? It fits.

MAMA, YO NO TENGO VISTO

Mother, I haven't seen him lately, I swear. And anyway, he has no power over me. He was just a Gypsy boy passing through. You said he was fire, but all I saw was smoke. And anyway, if anything, I'm water.

ENTRE LAS HUERTAS PASEANDO

Walking by the fields today, I heard a violin. It sounded like needlework in the air, it was that fine. A boy I had never seen was playing, sitting in the shade on a rock. He called to me. Said his name was Zion. What kind of name is that, *Zion?* I sat across from him, and he played for me, and what he played was slow and sweet, but as I sat there I felt blood, my own, and stood. Don't leave, he said, what is your name, he said. Call me *Morena*, I said, and I was gone. *Morena*, he called after me—you have one beautiful eye and one that scares me.

SION, TU MI OJO PRETO

Zion, my beautiful eye looks for you day after day. Three weeks now, forty-two times I've crossed the field, forty-two times I thought I heard violin, but it was just wind.

ALTA, ALTA ES LA LUNA

High, high the moon is tonight, far away. So white. There was a day when the moon was yellow, like peach skin, and I could have reached for it, held it to my chest, and I remember its face, troubled, in need of comfort. I should have held it to my chest.

EL REY QUE MUNCHO MADRUGA

The king who rises early gets his own food, Mother said. But I rise early today—I don't know why—and make breakfast for Mother. New bread, fresh eggs, tea. Silly girl, she says, why are you doing this? It's the first day of eternity, I tell her. You're so tan, she says, and touches me.

PAXARO D'HERMOZURA

Beautiful bird, you of the five colors, you of the yellow breast and black tail feathers, you of the pink neck and red shoulders, open your gray beak and speak: tell me Zion's real name.

AVRE TU PUERTA CERRADA

Open your closed door, I hear a quiet voice say. I go near the door, hear Zion's violin.

Mother is at the market, I say. I can't let you in.

AVRE ESTE ABAJOUR

Open this window, then, says Zion.

My window's already open, it's always open, but I'll say no more until you tell me your name.

I told you it's Zion, he says, but I stay silent. Zion, he says again, and plays his violin. Name, I say. *Spain*, he says, and I say Name! again and the sun freezes overhead. *Andarleto*, he says.

ANDARLETO, MI ANDARLETO

Andarleto, my Andarleto. So open the door now, you said, and I should have not done it. Mother was at the market, I should have not done it, but my body betrayed me. When mother returned it was almost night, and she had cherries and pears and apples. You seem so happy, she said. Is everything all right?

45

UNA PASTORA YO AMI

I loved a shepherd, I said, and it was a stupid thing to say, I could see that right away. A girl? Mother said. No, a boy, I said. You used the feminine, Mother said. I guess I was nervous, I said, and anyway it was just kisses.

Oh, good, she said, what a relief.

Some mothers have a way of taking air from you and not giving it back. Mother's not like that. She knows no one owns the air. But I lied to her.

YO ME ACODRO D'AQUELLA NOCHE

I remember the night Nani lied to Mother. There were no cherries, no apples or pears. Just some yelling, harsh words, many tears. My own tears, too, fell from my eyes, though I did not know why. Lies! Mother kept saying. Lies!

DON AMADI

Don Amadi came calling. He is a farmer who has a big, dull son. This cannot be, I thought. Andarleto, does a lie come so quickly with punishment, did your Zion, your Spain, my talk of kisses bring this on?

I hope you're enjoying my pears, Don Amadi said to Mother. Ah, this is not about me. This is about her.

DURME, DURME

Sleep, sleep, worried self. There is no wind tonight. The lights from the harbor are there, the air is clean, and Don Amadi and Mother laugh in the other room. It is so good to hear Mother laughing. Andarleto, what I gave you yesterday I will give you tomorrow, the next day—as many times as there are needles of pine.

ADIOS QUERIDA

Goodbye, my dear, I hear Mother say. Does a lie cancel another lie? Was Mother at the market yesterday? Don Amadi said goodbye in the old way, formal, respectful. And then he sneezed! How they laughed! Oh Mother, if you could only know the joys we share these days. I know that Nani is my sister, but tonight you and I are sisters, too.

ESTA MONTAÑA D'ENFRENTE

This mountain across the way has always seemed to me a woman sleeping. When it is late, when the mountain is dark blue against the sky, you can see her head thrown back, her breasts, her big hips, even the feet—bent to the side—those clumps of pines we hike through. I've always thought she was from across the water, Africa, but tonight maybe she is me. Andarleto and I spent time in those pines today.

CASCAVELA DEL AMOR

Bells of love from the church. Someone is getting married. Let their love ring, let their love last, let no dark clouds like high waves rear up on them. Today, I have no thought of getting married. I think to eat the pears, not grow them. Maybe this will change.

LA COMIDA DE LA MAÑANA

The morning meal in which I will tell Mother. I have cooked eggs again, but with pepper and onion, more spicy than before. And the tea stronger. Mother, I am leaving for Marseille, I say. Leaving for Marseille? she says. She is not as shocked as I thought she'd be. I must look for Nani, I say. And how will you go there, dear one: you'll need money. Andarleto has money, I say.

And who, may I ask, is Andarleto?

Mother, those days you've spent with Don Amadi have been good days for me.

YENDOME PARA MARSILIA

Leaving for Marseille. What is Marseille? I have heard that it, too, is on the sea, that there are candles in windows everywhere, and fishing boats heavy with every fish, great fires in winter, and men with white shoes, women with dresses you can see through. I don't care if none of it is true. Andarleto will be here tomorrow.

MI SUEGRA

My mother-in-law lives in Marseille, Mother says. Doña is a good woman. Here is the name of her street. Go there if trouble finds you. Tell her who you are. They say her house is on a hill, like ours, and overlooks the harbor.

I ask Mother if Nani stays with her mother-in-law. Oh, no, Mother says. If Nani is still there, she will not be with her. Nani has a mind of her own.

LAS ESTRELLAS DE LOS CIELOS

The stars of the sky are your sugar, the moon the milk in your tea. All the sky is for you, dear. Mother used to sing that to me, and she comes tonight to my bed, sings it in a tone deeper than I remember.

YA VIENE EL CATIVO

The captive is coming tomorrow, she says. What do you mean, I say. She runs her hand through my hair the way she used to. If I'd just washed it sometimes I didn't like that, but tonight I do. What do you mean, I say, about the captive, and Mother says, He thinks he has captivated you, this Andarleto, he and his violin. But even good men don't understand. He is your captive, and it will take him ten years to know this. Ten if he has a good map. Ten if he doesn't drink raki.

LA VIDA DO POR EL RAQUI

I gave my life for raki. That is what Father said when I saw him at the harbor before he died. I never told that to Mother.

HIJA MIA MI QUERIDA

My daughter, my dear, says Mother, you are a brave girl, and I admire you. Know that I am with you wherever you go. Keep your life. Remember those almond blossoms on the hill in Málaga? Even in times of war, they come back. Every year. They are still there, my almond blossom.

I did not understand what Mother meant.

UNA NOCHE AL LUNAR

On a full-moon night, late, Andarleto came for me. Silvana didn't think he would, but he did. He put a silver chain around my neck and pulled it, gently. You're my prisoner, he said. We'll see about that, I said. Marseille is a long way, he said, we should start.

It is hard to speak of my goodbyes. I will only say that I love it that Andarleto kissed Mother. Take care of my little flower, she said.

I will, he said.

AVRIX MI GALANICA

Open, my pretty one, Andarleto said as he lay me on the blanket in our first field on our way out of town. I opened for him. The moon shone on my new chain.

UNA TARDE FRESQUITA DE MAYO

A cool afternoon in May, Marseille, and I hear music in the street that is harsh, more than I can bear. Bear down, the woman says, my hair soaked with sweat, twelve hours in this place and nothing, Andarleto leaving, arriving, leaving, arriving, and I see that he, too, has been weeping.

MADRE, SI YO ME MUERO

Mother, if I die in this brutal house with this stern nurse, know that I still wear the silver chain and that Andarleto wears a gold one. Know that even if my eyes are blind with sweat I can see almond flowers.

DURME, DURME HERMOZO HIJICO

Sleep, sleep, beautiful son, *nuevo Andarleto, Andarletito*. Soon we will be in our own bed, your father beside us. Sleep, beautiful son, blackest of hair on your clay-colored head.

MAMA MIA MI QUERIDA

My mother, my dear, men in uniforms have come to our
house seeking Andarleto, speaking rudely, commanding. They
say he must join them if we are to remain in Marseille. It
seems I will be a soldier soon, he says, but maybe not for long.

ESCUCHIS SEÑOR SOLDADO

Listen, Mister Soldier: don't let them take you. Andarleto
needs a father, I need a lover. One war is just like another.
White skeletons are not white flowers.

MAMA MIA MI QUERIDA

My mother, my dear, they did not tell him first, but took him.
They took him from a street close to here, his friends say. No
goodbyes.

DIZIOCHO AÑOS TENGO

I am eighteen years old, lost in Marseille with a little boy. Our
comrade struggled to come home, his friends said. He tried to
make it, but they saw him in the pines.

His gold chain longer than my silver; it hangs deeper on
my chest. Who is the captive now, Mother?

LA CALEJA DE MATALON

The alley of Matalon is full of women, and holds no homes overlooking the harbor. I saw Nani standing in the alley, Mother. It was cold, but her blouse was thin. At last, I said, and put my hands on her shoulders. She did not recognize me. When I told her who I was, she looked away. I saw her there again and again, but each time I approached she walked away. More of my heart is broken.

Doña remembers you, Mother, and sends her regards. You were a wonderful teacher for her son, she says, but he did not take the lesson. She will find a man for me, she says, and let fate do the rest. She is so good to my son.

DOS AMANTES TENGO, MAMA

I have two lovers, Mother: the one I never married inside me, and he who every night gets on top of me. We are in a new place now, with lavender, bees, a place looking over the harbor. I had heard that it was wonderful to have two lovers.

TUS OJICOS JOYA MIA

Your eyes are my jewels—that's what I said to little Andarleto when he asked why I didn't have stones hung from my chains. You should see his eyes, Mother. We will visit soon, I promise. I have some money. We will go to the inn with the hanging lanterns.

OH, QUE HERMOZA MUCHACHA

Oh, what a pretty young lady—that's what the man on the seawall said when I passed him after market. Men like that called me *Morena*, I remembered, but this one was without respect, he offered me money, said I should go with him, and of course I did not, would not. Though my son Andarleto was not with me, his hand was in my hand.

—in memory of Jorge Liderman

3

Crucifixion, Kinetic

OFTEN, THE SCENE depicted as tranquil—fait accompli, three men in their proper places, on crosses, assorted provokers and grievers below, sky leaden, sense overall not meat but vegetal, varnished, *tableau*.

Let's say it did occur.

Then: *cross?* This planed and surfaced lumber in pictures we knew long ago—in Giotto, Raphael, even Goya?

No. Rough spar. Oak. Or cedar. Maybe an adze hacked away the bark, maybe a few draw-knife marks, but it's still tree, still round, chunks of its skin left on, bleeding sap, lots of knots—strong enough, though, to hold a man.

Each upright so tall no mother at night might take down a son, no brother a brother. And the cross-strut surely not mortised, fit tight/square to its vertical other, but cruder stuff: hemp-rope to lash the X together, coarse fiber, the cross-strut at front, main beam behind, rope laps raising it farther so that a man's deltoids and pectoralis majors are either racked backwards, spine arched out from the upright, or else his arms straight, pinned at wrists and elbows, thoracic vertebrae torqued inward, rolled; he's hunchbacked.

The tying's done on the ground, of course, crowd gathered 'round, a few protesting at first, most goading, quick-tempered, spinning to kick dogs fighting underfoot.

And of the three: do they accede, span themselves over each cross? Not likely.

Struggle, boots to the gut, the men blindsided, bare-knuckled, yanked down, faces struck and kicked, clothes ripped, and their cursing—all three, and all three self-mucused and bloodied and pissed, pinned now at the wrists, ankles crossed and bound, four soldiers to a man, *More rope! More rope!* Knives tossed to slice the hemp, and they're stilled now, fixed, the crowd cheering *Yes!*—one of the men in the crowd with a hard-on.

Some few curse the soldiers, their epithets kept under breath.

Three tall crosses, one by one to be raised.

Who dug these goddamn holes? Not deep enough! One-third the length of each pole! Who trained you fools—your mothers?

And the laborers, new men, bend again, fifteen minutes' work, their blades shear rock, much complaint, the tied men still supine, new rubble beside the postholes, and now the call to raise: a soldier at each side of the struts, two at the vertical, they count, lift, the wet wood heavy and the bound man heavy, no balance to be had, pitching backward, swaying, *Lift higher!* says one with a helmet on, and the cross is lifted, lowered into its hole, voice of man on pole dolorous and lost in the crowd, but still it's not plumb, *It's leaning,* and they heave too far left, foolish workmen, compensate now too far right, finally straight, the workmen shamed, angry, *There— now fill it in*, shovelers packing rubble into the hole, slapping it with the back of their blades, the pole-holding soldiers still shouldering it, heroic poses in opposition to each other, more rubble, more soil. *Done. Next one.*

The second one plumbed, and now to the third man, still on the ground, bound, the one they were told to nail. The nails flat-shafted, pounded on an anvil, tapered, black. The man's right wrist bound tight, one nail straight through the capitatum. *That's no pain*, they say, *you woman. Want nails in the tips of your fingers?* Now the left.

The man's feet, wrong in literature and tableau, here crossed at the ankles, bound in hemp, loosed briefly so that each crossed foot can find a surface for nailing. Two men on their knees—each takes a foot, jerks it downward, works it around the side of the post, nails it in. The cord tightened again.

The man himself now, as if oiled: in blood, in sweat, in piss, and the noises he makes animal noises, inhuman. He is raised, the skies leaden, yes, the birds already circling, the soldiers folding their arms, well pleased.

Companionship,

SHE'D WRITTEN, *certainly at first,* and he'd answered—
wanted to meet early—*so okay, we'll meet at 8 a.m.,* she wrote,
and at least this is no lazy man, and she came at eight, the
café up the hill by, what was it—a memorial to some soldiers,
some war?—and he was already there in the blue pullover
cap about which he'd written ("pillover," he'd really written),
and he had coffee in front of him and waved and stood,
proper gentleman, shook her hand, ordered her coffee like a
proper man, and his English was good, and he paid, and she
liked the tip he left and the hand that left the tip—tanned,
delicate black hairs on the fingers—and she liked his voice,
you could be in radio, she told him, and let's walk, he said,
this is your first week in your new city, *my* city, I love this
city, and they walked and walked, he showed her the old
cathedral, *my* church, he said, every Sunday, he said, and the
old Justice Palace, and up the hill, hard to keep up (his long,
strong legs), up to where the crazy writer lived and died and
down an alley then where two famous lovers had their trysts,
and it was then he first put his hand on her shoulder, briefly

only, but she liked it very much, and he took her to where the artists live, so-and-so lives there, he's a sculptor, so-and-so lives there, she's a performance artist, and it was always *dare* instead of *there*, like a little boy, then down the hill and up another to the botanical garden, where he must have known the name of every tree—he called them by men's names first—very funny, she said, then came the Latin, his ease with Latin, genus/family/species, and then it was time for lunch, I know a good place for lunch, he said, it's just below the garden, it's a good day, he said, we can sit outside, and lunch was delicious, she had lamb, he had oysters, and the waiters knew him, playful with him, called him Professor—damn, he's handsome, she thought, and said I'll pay, and *no no no*, he said, and *yes yes*, she said, I insist—then he took her to the famous open market at the base of the hill then to the river, which was clean now, he said, the fish are back, then down the promenade beside the river to the old mill, do you have more energy, he said, it's your new city, he said, sure, she said, but she was getting tired, and oh, I like this man, she thought, the way he touches my hand and does not hold it, he understands respect, and now they came upon the photo gallery, and they went in and he liked the same ones as she and pointed out others she would not have noticed, then out the door and off to the cross-section of the ancient city wall, then around the corner, the leatherworkers' alley, over two more to the silversmiths', then past the House of Chocolates where he bought her something orange and aromatic with what—cardamom? and then through the flower stands, where he bought her a yellow rose—wise, too early for red, she thought—though she was really ready for red, I'd better stop now, she said, I'd better go, and can I see you again, she wanted him to say, but it was then that he asked for money, and it was a large amount of money, an amount that confused her, and she said *what* and she said *why* and she said *no* and she said *why* again and he said for the city tour, beach, but they had seen no beach, and oh, it's *bitch*, he's calling me *bitch* and I'll call the police, she said, and he said call the police, I know the police, and she looked around, and she was not in an alley, she was on a city corner, but it was deserted just now, and he called her *beach* again, and took out his phone and said *he* would call the police, and it wasn't worth it, it just wasn't worth it, his accent thickening, a drunkenness in it now though he was not drunk, and she reached into her purse and gave him all the money she had, and he took it, and did not stuff it into his pockets and run, but bill by bill, carefully, tenderly, slid each into his wallet and closed it and said thank you, now be careful, this is a dangerous city.

Pasencore

The town seemed a good place to stay on our way from Basel to Bologna, so we marked it on the map, headed up the pass—rugged outcrops, spruce dusted with fresh snow—and after an hour's drive on the serpentine two-lane road we saw the town sign: *Pasencore*, and pulled into a gas station. I got out and walked into the little office to give the attendant my money. ENGLISH SPOKEN, said a sign on the counter, and after a month struggling with German, I was grateful.

"*Pasencore*," I said, "that's a strange name for a town—is it named after someone?"

The clerk, a corpulent post-adolescent eating potato chips, shrugged.

"What'd you find out?" my wife said after I pumped gas and got into the car.

"Nothing. Not much English."

We dropped down to the center of town and saw a hotel—newly painted trim, bright brass sign, eased into its parking lot. The staff couldn't have been more kind: unloading our bags, showing us the way to the front desk. We checked in,

the desk clerk almost fawningly polite, and when I compli-
mented him on his English and the attentiveness of the staff,
he averted his eyes, held up his hand, and said, "Please, sir,
no . . ." a gesture I took as a vestige, in this ancient town, of the
lost art of hoteliers' modesty, deferential but unobsequious.

"Pasencore—is it named after someone?" I asked.

"Oh, no, sir. A very old name. Hundreds of years."

I let it go.

We were shown to our room. It was simple, comfort-
able. My wife leafed through brochures on the desk and
noticed that the great German soprano Sie Flohschnell
was performing that evening at the rococo concert hall we'd
passed on the way down the hill. We decided to go.

We ate dinner in the hotel dining room—the waitress
excellent but eccentric. She refused our tip, saying only,
"Thank you sincerely yours, but I must love this town."

Arriving at the hall fifteen minutes early, we saw that we
were underdressed. I had on a coat and tie, my wife her black
traveling dress, but clearly Flohschnell's performing here was
momentous, and I sensed my wife's embarrassment in the
midst of the town's women, who wore jewels and evening
gowns. We were travelers, though, confident that we'd be
obvious as such and forgiven, though some of the men in
their stiff tuxedoes did send haughty looks my way.

The program looked ambitious. Bach's "Meine Beine sind
stark," Schumann's "Mutter, Mutter, erschreckende Nacht,"
and others, without intermission, ending in Brahms's "Aber
sie zahlen so viel." My wife remembered having read last

year that Flohschnell had sneezed too hard one morning, ruptured a blood vessel in a vocal cord, and might not ever sing again. That explained, perhaps, the crowd's palpable air of anticipation.

The accompanist strode out, sans applause, flipped his coattail behind him in the old flourish as he sat. Then Flohschnell emerged, again to no applause, wearing a red satin dress, a necklace of blue stones, the proper operatic cleavage, and oddly, what women call "comfortable shoes"— this version black, in no way matching the outfit, but surely the practical accoutrement for arduous road trips.

She sang a flawless Bach, as if the old meter master were at her side. Schumann's "Mutter, Mutter" was subtle and poetic. All the way through, the program went fluidly, the accompanist almost seeming part of Flohschnell, sewn to her—he was that sensitive. The crowd, clearly in awe, awaiting the denouement, held its applause and made little guttering sounds after each number—not the *mmm* we were used to, but what might be called a pleasurable growl.

Then came the denouement: Brahms's monumental "Aber sie zahlen," sung with such plangency that my wife and I were brought to tears, the crowd rapt, on the edge of their seats, Flohschnell's voice breaking a bit at the end—had she planned it?—as if in that single broken note all the fear, all the foreboding contained in the song were manifest in the soprano herself. Quite a coda.

My wife and I had expected the entire hall—already on edge—to burst to their feet, *Brava! Brava!* and *Encore!* And the full-bodied soprano, still flushed with the power of Brahms, to take a breath, bow, leave the stage, return to a cascade of applause—no problems with *that* voice!—then, once more, sing.

Instead, at the last note the accompanist leapt to his feet, took the crook of Flohschnell's left arm, and swept her offstage, the two of them hurrying, the crowd now standing, surging forward as one, absolutely without applause, and chasing them. Some vaulted onto the stage, some took the stairs, not a single seat still filled except ours, the crowd clotted stage right—the exit Flohschnell had taken—jostling each other to join the chase.

My wife and I were stunned. "Let's go," I said.

"Yes!" she said, and as I stepped toward the stage, she said "No, home—to the hotel!" and I said, "Oh, no—I have to see this."

I bullied her into joining me, pulling her along. We were at the back of the crowd, which progressed quickly down a dimly lit backstage corridor skeletoned with equipment. The crowd was resolute, remarkably quiet, mostly the sound of footsteps, occasionally those earlier guttering noises, repressed, and the corridor led to another, then another, thinner, dimmer, the *sussing* sound of fancy dresses, leather shoes on wooden floors, and the guttering again, and soon we were out the door and into the street, the entire audience hurtling up the cobblestone road ascending from the town, and in the distance, near the top of the hill, I could see the soprano high-stepping, her gown hiked, red underwear ablaze, the accompanist beside her, urging her on, the crowd gaining.

We were horrified, but kept running. At the top of the hill, the soprano and her piano man dove into the back seat of a waiting limousine, the car accelerated, lost traction for a moment, gained it again, gone.

The crowd simply sighed a great collective sigh, turned, and wordlessly—though the sound of five hundred high heels on cobblestone, like a spilled bucket of ball bearings, will always remain with me—returned to town.

"What was *that* about?" my wife said, as we descended in the crisp night air toward our hotel. "Maybe something about the history of Germans around here," I said.

We decided to stay awhile. We had time; the mountains were lovely, spring not far off, and the next night we went to hear the symphony in that same hall.

An odd symphony it was. All piccolos, flutes, clarinets, trumpets, and violins. Not a French horn, no tuba, no contrabass, no cello, no bassoon. Why was that—were they afraid of depth here, of grief?

Soon, we discovered the reason. The playing was lovely— all the upper-register stuff they could find, apparently: mostly baroque. And again, the no applause/musicians sprinting away, instruments in hand, down the shabby caverns of the old hall, out into the street, the crowd in hot chase breathing at their necks, the exhausted lungs at the top of the cobblestone street, a bus waiting this time, both doors open, ladders up to the emergency windows, the bus full in seconds, the ladders drawn in, the bus gone in a black blast of diesel, the collective sigh, the crowd's descent, mute as the night before.

"They bring only what instruments they can run with," my wife said, somewhat undone, as we headed back to the hotel to get a drink. I ordered a double.

The next night, jazz. A club downtown. House piano, a quintet: alto sax, ukulele, cornet, bongo drums.

"This is jazz—what's with the bongo drums?" I said to my wife.

Applause-less night again, eerie, and we didn't know that the last number would be the last. It was an up-tempo version of Paolo Conte's "Corrono velocemente, idioti," the sax woman playing solo, the piano rocking, the sax woman dancing offstage, bobbing down the aisle of the dark club, the crowd rocking, too, then the ukulele, quick-fingered, edgy, now the cornet man, glasses and close-cropped hair, bringing his bright horn down into the audience, call and response with the piano, the uke lady in answer from the side aisle, and at last the bongo boy holding his little drums above his head, fingers quick on their skin, the boy leaping up, striding the middle aisle, the whole place rocking, while the piano man, standing, brought it *almost* home, then quit—one bar short, yelled "Jiggers!" and ditched, the five taking different exits, the crowd splitting five ways, and the ritual merging on the cobblestone path to the top of the town, motorcycles waiting, great roar, deep sigh, crowd home.

We were addicted: stayed, saw it all: the Russian ballet dancers doing *Swan Lake*, the specter of those ladder-thin figures sprinting up the street in their tutus and ballet shoes, Siegfried in the lead, Odette's feathers flying everywhere, the crowd in their own frenzied dash seemingly silent, too, as if wanting to luxuriate in the sound of those malleable ballet shoes on their ancient streets . . . Then Tuesday night the poet, who tried what must be an old trick in Pasencore, saying he'd end with two more poems but vaulting from the stage in the middle of poem one, the pitiful spectacle of his climbing the hill—so clear it'd been years since he'd run—and no car waiting as he crested it and sprinted downward, out of town.

We'd had enough experience with reticence here to know not to ask *why*. But that last night, that poet night, I had to ask the desk clerk at the hotel the question my wife and I had pondered for five nights now.

"Why don't they ever catch them?" I demanded. "I mean, the sopranos are so slow, poets can hardly handle a hill, and—"

He stopped me. Gave me a level look.

"Oh, we don't do that here, sir. We may have our queer history, but we are a dignified people."

We slept unsettled, woke at three, and left quietly.

Audio Guide:
The Paintings You Missed

LET US MOVE NOW to the painting at the opposite end of this great room.

Though untitled and unsigned, this work has been attributed to the French painter Jean-Baptiste Greuze. Even if its provenance does indeed trace to Greuze, it's certain that he would never have signed it. Clearly, the subject in the massive bed is a king—note the rocaille furniture and royal accoutrements around him, the servants-in-waiting gathered around the bed. He's in his royal nightshirt, and, shockingly, headless. But note that there is no blood to be seen—and that he holds, angled toward him, an ornate but *empty* frame. And this is where the genius of this painting lies: the frame surely represents a mirror, and in its emptiness we viewers see *through*—see what the mirror itself would see: a king whose head has been severed cleanly—almost surgically. There is yet a second compelling level in this painting: the implicit sense of dialogue among his attendants—a feeling that the king's words still hover in the air, as if he has asked a question: perhaps, *How do I look?* And the chamber-servants seem to be replying, the painter inviting us to fill in the dialogue. *You look as well as can be expected, Majesty, but you'll carry on,* one might be saying. How completely the painting allows our participation! And note, too, before we leave, its sense of the "caught moment," of an almost Dutch realism: a section of golden cathedral visible through the window behind the headless king, the cathedral suffused in the same golden light that fills the chamber. But note that the cathedral has no cross on its steeple, suggesting, perhaps, that it is not a cathedral at all but the worshipping place of a faith outside Christianity.

So, if this is the work of Greuze—and our art historians believe that it is—we can imagine the danger our artist might have been in had he signed it, its heavy sarcasm threatening any monarchy, especially a dying one.

Proceed now to the next room, to the painting looming before you on the east wall. Press Number 17 when you arrive.

This painting has not been exhibited before—partly, of course, because of the challenges of its size: you can see that it covers almost the entire wall. In fact, when first painted by Géricault, seven years before his untimely death—he fell from a horse in 1824—it dominated his studio for months, until at last he rolled up the canvas and stored it away. Géricault never exhibited this painting, preferring to tour with his later *The Raft of the Medusa*—a work of similar size. This piece, which he simply called *The Raft*, was an early study.

We witness a raft speeding toward the rapids of a wide river, a city dimly outlined on the receding far bank. The raft is packed with soldiers peering into the current, clearly fatigued, soaked, heavy in their uniforms.

Then we notice the feature of this painting that caused Géricault ultimately to hold back the work, and prompted later executors to exert the same judgment. If we look closely, we see that the raft itself is of unmistakably phallic shape, slightly curved, rich in tonal variegation, even the vague outline of what seems a scrotum at the aft, serving, it seems, as buoyancy device for its cargo of benumbed warriors, the raft's trajectory into the spume inevitable. Is Géricault commenting, perhaps, on the true nature of war— suggesting, it, too, is a biological imperative? We don't know, but the painting certainly suggests it.

Even today, this work has created controversy. For numerous reasons, the museum's board has decided to shorten its exhibition, and it will return to storage at the end of the month.

Proceed now to the small alcove just to the right of the Géricault, and press Number 18.

This striking work is a triptych on wood, painted, certainly, as an *homage* to Pietro Lorenzetti's medieval *Birth of the Virgin*. It is complex, but our attention to its detail will be rewarded.

The center panel is tallest, carved in the shape of a Gothic arch, flanked on each side by similar arches, each shorter than that in the center. Notice that the scrollwork on the arches is painted with gold leaf, and note, too, the trompe l'oeil of three-dimensional stone as each arch curves into its lower verticality.

Ah, but we viewers of the twenty-first century see that that is where the fourteenth century ends—for this triptych is a newly discovered work by the late American artist George Bellows, a controlled but tumultuous oil in the tradition of his *Stag at Sharkey's*. Its icon-like structure suggests ceremony, and the ritual delivered here, as in *Stag*, is contemporary— this time, though, not a boxing match, but a wrestling match in a big-city auditorium.

The left panel, narrower than the center, shows, standing in one corner, a corpulent wrestler in a mitred hat. His golden robe reads THE PONTIFF, and his attendant, in red, massaging his shoulders, resembles early renderings of Cardinal Richelieu. In the opposing corner, we see a gaunt and robeless wrestler cowering. He has a tattoo on his right shoulder, and if you're able to stand closely enough to make it out, note that it says MONTESQUIEU, the scowling audience behind him all cardinals in pointed red hats.

We look at the middle panel, clearly the main event, holding all the freneticism we remember from Bellows's work. The pope is now stripped of his robe, his mitre propped on the corner post, his skin shining with oil (note the bottle marked PAPAL UNCTION in his corner, its cross-shaped stopper). He's blindingly white, roll on roll of soft flesh, he's moving toward Montesquieu, his beatific smile tinged with menace, arms spread in evangelical religiosity, and we see

Montesquieu anxiously glancing at his attendant behind the ropes. Some art historians have said that the attendant resembles John Locke, but others have disagreed. The attendant points at his own head, as if to say, *Think, man, think!* Note the lack of definition in Montesquieu's outline, Bellows perhaps foreshadowing what is to come. In the background, we note another section of the audience: Ku Klux Klansmen in pointed white hats.

Finally, the denouement, the panel on the right. The wrestlers are on the mat, the pope's corpulence almost completely covering Montesquieu—only Montesquieu's wild hair and splayed legs visible from under the pontiff's holy mass. Note how Bellows, with single flecks of pigment, suggests the profusion of the papal perspiration—almost cartoon-like. The referee, his face clearly that of Mussolini—bends over the wrestlers, a finger raised, signifying *one*. Montesquieu's time on the mat, it seems, has just begun.

And note, finally, the third section of spectators: artists, musicians, writers. A quick, deft caricature of van Gogh in the front row, sketchbook in hand, Chopin and George Sand necking at the back, three identical versions of Gertrude Stein seated throughout, a sallow Edgar Allan Poe, Mahler moping beside him, Weegee crouched ringside in black and white—his camera focused—and in the aisle, the exact likeness of Baudelaire, standing, staring toward the red exit sign.

Proceed now to the adjoining Blue Room, where awaiting us is a canvas Hieronymus Bosch is said to have painted from his deathbed, "his brush thrashing, dipping in red, dripping in red, spreading the red as if he himself had become both fire and fuel," as the painter's son wrote in his journal. Press Pause now, then Number 19 when you arrive at the image of the figure with the rucksack rushing from the flaming house on the hill.

The Extraordinary
Accordionist

MARIO BADIO SET UP under a lamp post at the center of the square. Tourist groups sometimes passed there on the way to see the Romanesque church down the hill, and if even a few groups came that day, and from each group if ten kind souls tossed coins into his case, that would be a good day.

The residents around the square were accustomed to buskers—this, the prettiest place in town—*Musicians have a right to make their living, don't they?* they'd say—but the bad music that rose to their windows was sometimes more than they could bear: fiddle notes like tin being torn, inattentive guitar, flutes whose bamboo seemed to yearn for their forest.

So when *this* accordionist sat on the bench under the lamp post, lit a cigarette, uncased his old Scandalli Polifonico with its forty-one black and white keys, its hundred-and-twenty bright celluloid buttons, its hand-carved reeds, the eighteen folds of its bellows, when his shoulder strap was snug and his bass strap tight, nothing was out of the ordinary: the hotel maids hurried to clean the disheveled rooms, the waiter at the café on the square moved quickly to set his outdoor tables for lunch, and the square itself was almost empty, only an old man on a bench lifting his face to the sun.

Mario Badio shoved his cigarette to the side of his mouth and began to play. He started slowly—a gentle French waltz, "L'indifférence" and though anyone familiar with accordionists knows that it takes a few tunes to get the blood flowing, in "L'indifférence" it was as if his trudge up the hill were enough, and his fingers across the keys and over the Braille of bass buttons traveled lightly, with a dexterity that seemed to belie the man's hands themselves: short, stout fingers, rough—the hands of a workingman.

He played with "L'indifférence" awhile, staring, reporting the tune once straight through, then again, this time decorated, rococo, then yet again, now abstracting the waltz, disornamenting it, atonal. The waiter setting tables stopped and turned his way.

No one was near Badio: no tour groups passing, and the old man at the side of the square had turned his angular face slightly in the direction of the music, but only slightly.

Badio brought "L'indifférence" home now, saddening it in drawn musettes and single bellow shakes, ending with a dolefulness the waiter had never heard, and, still turned in the accordionist's direction, he called out over his shoulder to two women in the kitchen.

The accordionist's coin case was empty, but that didn't seem to concern him.

He played "La Foule" next, an old Southern French song about a crowd dancing an insane farandole, a man and a woman losing each other in that crowd. It's a waltz: 3/4 time, and Mario Badio played it that way, then came 'round again and quickened it, and soon the maids in the hotel leaned from the windows, and the desk clerk stepped into the square in her high heels and floral skirt, and the old man turned fully as Badio's velocity increased, double bellow shakes, triple, and all around the square, windows thrown open, and though the sun went behind a cloud and the stone square went cold, it didn't seem to matter to the accordionist or to his new audience, who, once he finished the mad farandole, burst into applause, to which applause he nodded, subtly, then without pause launched into the great Russian "Black Eyes"—"Les Yeux Noirs" to the people of that town, and the town had never heard such a thing, this mournful overture, first played French-café style, oversweet, then as if *traveling* the tune, taking it country by country, version by version from Turkey to Russia, the journey urgent, Badio never once extending his bellows dramatically the way some do, the bellows so controlled one would have thought they were his own lungs—and perhaps they were, for he was a long-distance player, this one, and ten minutes into those black *yeux* the sun came out again, the square ablaze with light, with the new gold of chestnut trees, and by now everyone within earshot was in the square: the maids and the waiter and kitchen workers, the fifth-floor residents and the fourth, the buildings emptying, the old man standing now, the astounded crowd not *approaching* Badio but by their numbers brought closer to him as he played and played, and it was difficult to distinguish his fingers from the shadow of his fingers in the sun, it was all so fast. What range! What crescendo, decrescendo! The bellows quivering like violin tremolos, oh Badio pulled music out of that machine like no one ever had, he was at fifteen minutes now, and the waiter and the cook began to dance on the ochre paving stones, and of course the dance spread, and by the time "Les Yeux" was in its twentieth minute, bass buttons flashing in the sun, the whole square was dancing, trios, couples, singles, and in one magnificent glissando Badio brought it to an end.

Applause, of course. Coins tossed into the case.

That was all. The accordionist smiled, nodded again, and, having played for an hour, stopped. The sun went behind a cloud, neighbors and workers went inside, and the musician snapped his accordion away and crossed the square toward the subway.

At around two a group of tourists came, their guide asking them to pause a moment to notice the square's almost preternatural serenity, pointing out to them the figure of an old man on a bench in the far corner, his face inclined toward the sun, his angular features remarkably like those of Giacometti.

Gesture

HE'D HAD TWO PINTS of Guinness at O'Doul's down the street before the play, walked a block to the theater, stopped in at the bathroom, then taken his seat in the balcony.

All week, the Irishman had been looking forward to it: Joyce's "The Dead," whose subtlety had meant so much to him in college days.

But when he went that night, fortified, he was disappointed: a mealy-mouthed Gabriel—the lead, bearer of the narrative—mewling into the footlights; a big cast spewing songs in butchered Irish accents that sounded more like perverted Serbian, all Joycean subtlety lost in a morass of words incomprehensible to him at his height.

And so it was that he began, in his disappointment, to focus on the couple in front of him. She: thin, wearing a leopard-print dress, earringed with silver globes, her dark bronze hair cut into a sharp ducktail. And the man much older, balding, his head shining in the backlight of the exit sign, gray hair wisping over one ear, his coat a checked pattern that clashed with his partner's dress.

At the third song, she leaned slightly forward, her torso a leopard triangle in the flat light. Her companion reached over and put his hand on her neck—too mechanically, the Irishman thought—and began massaging gently as the song went on.

It was "Three Jolly Pigeons," he recognized—a stamping of feet to a fife whose fifer only mimed the instrument, a half-beat behind a recording's rising strains.

Clearly, the woman was enjoying the massage, and when as the song ended her companion withdrew his hand, she continued rotating her head as if missing the hand, as if in pain from an injury long unmended.

It was then that the Irishman, diminished in his hope for the prospect of a tender rendering of Joyce, reached forward his own hand and began massaging.

It seemed so natural: the top vertebrae below the neck familiar, the muscles at each side like tight cords to a window shade, the kneading necessary.

Some time passed, quiet, meditative, and then he was startled to hear her companion's words—loud in that intimate dark—each word truncated, disassociated: "*What. Are. You. Doing?*" And the woman in the leopard dress turning in confusion, her eyes wide, her mouth open, saying nothing.

And the Irishman then not withdrawing his hand, but keeping it there at the nub of her neck—a testament, he hoped, to his kind intention, then, ever so slowly, beginning its withdrawal, the other man creating a disturbance now in the dimness (the cast below fully engulfed in the distant music of "Parnell's Plight"), again asking "*What are you doing?*" and the Irishman, sensing eyes all around upon him, feeling a need to respond, withdrawing his hand more quickly, putting it in his lap, covering it now with his other hand, speaking:

"It was just . . . a gesture," he said, weakly, and remembered leaning over O'Connell Bridge one wet night, a white horse behind him pulling an empty tourist carriage, the Liffey's filthy waters flowing below.

"I'm sorry," said the Irishman to the woman's companion, the woman by now bending her head into her hands as if in another sort of pain, the Irishman amazed at what a night this had been—as the woman's companion now stood, turned toward him, and the cast below began its feeble version of Joyce's own song: "Rain on Rahoon Falls Softly . . ."

An Honest Cup of Coffee

ONCE A STUDENT at a university decided he'd spend a year studying overseas in a country he'd read about but never visited. He flew to the country's capital, took a room in the dormitories—a view of the river—and immersed himself in its beauty, its difficult language, its argumentative and passionate people.

In the school cafeteria, the young man would often sit across from a fellow student he didn't know and blithely start a conversation, although the tradition was that no conversations between strangers—even strangers who had come from other countries—would take place during mealtimes. But his behavior, wide-eyed, seemed to shock his chosen partners into a kind of generosity, even effusion. Soon, he had many friends who greeted him as he passed their table.

One morning, he went out to buy some notebooks and decided, despite his budget, to treat himself to coffee at the counter of a little café. He ordered his coffee using the proper words in their proper order, but the proprietor claimed not to understand him, and twice the young man had to repeat.

The coffee came, the young man thanked him and drank it, and when the proprietor, a big man with black hair and a belly like a balloon, saw that he was finished, he demanded twice the price the young man had read on the tariff card outside.

"Wait a minute," said the young man in his own language, forgetting where he was. "That's twice what it says out there." He went to his dictionary then, found the word for *double*, said it emphatically, then pointed to the tariff card in the window. All the while the proprietor held out his upturned palm.

"No," the young man said, and stated the amount of money on the tariff card, and tried to say, again with the help of his dictionary, that he'd seen the man next to him, who had coffee no different from his, pay exactly what was on the card—not even a tip left on the counter. Still, the proprietor held out his fleshy hand.

The young man shrugged his shoulders, reached into his pocket, and paid.

As he walked away, he felt shamed. First, to allow himself a spontaneous cup of coffee at all was extravagant—and second, in having paid double, he'd lost twice the money he never should have spent in the first place.

All day the incident bothered him, and when at dinner in the school cafeteria he got his tray and sat across from a pretty young woman who smiled at him, he said not a single word, deeply disturbed by what had occurred at the café.

Outside the cafeteria the young man saw some empty card-board boxes, and on the way up to his room he took one, and in his room took a large pair of scissors and cut two equal-sized rectangles from the box. On one, in tall letters, in his own language, he wrote: PLEASE DO NOT GO INTO THIS CAFÉ. THIS MAN CHEATED ME. HE CHARGED ME TWICE THE PRICE I SHOULD HAVE PAID FOR COFFEE. I JUST WANT MY MONEY BACK. THANK YOU.

"What are you doing?" his roommates asked.

"Oh, it's nothing. A private thing," he answered, and they were respectful, left him alone.

The other rectangle took longer. He did his best to write the same message in the language of the country he'd come to, but he was unsure of the accuracy of his grammar.

Then he found a stick and stapled the sign together: his own language on one side, the country's on the other, the stick just the right size for a handle.

The next morning, he went to the café and stood in front of it with his sign, walking slowly back and forth as he'd seen people of his own country do.

The café was near a subway stop, the street busy, filled with people hurrying to board their trains and go to work and make their money.

Even so, people slowed to read the young man's sign. And though he was certain of the righteousness of his cause, he was hurt to discover that those who stopped to read his sign made with their mouth a little twisted hissing sound—a sound he'd never heard before—and walked on. And those who entered the café shook their head at him and looked down.

After two hours, the young man, weary, disappointed, went to his classes.

But the next day, he awoke early and returned. He arrived just after the proprietor, who saw him pacing there with his sign and flung open the glass door and shouted something and slammed it.

Soon came the crowds along the sidewalk, again the hissings and *tsk*ings from a few, but now others—some of whom made those sounds yesterday—stopped in front of him and spoke, said things about the young man's country's behavior in a war long before he was born, its corrupt corporations, the sexual proclivities of its president.

To each of these the young man—by nature mild—simply shrugged, and it seemed that to spite him the haranguers would enter the café, whereas they might not have entered it yesterday. Soon the café was fuller than usual, and through the window the young man could see customers at the counter turning to stare at him as he paced—he could see the man with the belly like a balloon gesture toward him as he pulled the levers of the espresso machine or collected thick earthenware coffee cups from the counter.

For a few days, this went on. The man's business boomed; the young man was even spat at once, accused of inherent complicity in a distant bombing decades before.

But he stayed at it—went to his classes, studied, returned each early morning to the café.

Soon, the novelty wore off—not for him, but for the patrons. Though they held rancor toward his country, they developed a grudging respect for him—the manifestation of which began in the diminution of their invective, then progressed to their quickly nodding to him, then to their not entering the café on their way to the subway. Soon, it appeared to the young man that the proprietor's business was back to normal, that the boom days were over. He noticed that the proprietor, never having deigned to notice him since that first outburst at the front door, now glowered at him from behind the counter.

One morning, as was his habit, the young man arrived just minutes after the proprietor. The sky felt heavy—a downpour was predicted—and the young man hoped it wouldn't rain, because rain would wet his sign.

It was still dark, there were no customers yet, and in the yellow light of the café the young man saw the proprietor in his soiled white T-shirt straighten, bang his right fist on the counter, go to the cash register, open it, scoop up something, slam the drawer shut, and come to the door. Then he yanked the door wide, shouted some words at the young man— words that in his language meant *pig, money, luck*, tossed coins at the young man's feet with the motion of a habitual tosser of dice, and stood there at the door, his bare arms folded.

The young man wasn't sure what to do. The money he'd asked for was there at his feet. *I could reach down to get it and walk away*, he thought, *or I could infuriate him by pretending to have "found" some money, yet keep pacing with my sign. Or I could do nothing. But I'd better wait, and I'd better think, because I don't know what to do.*

At just that moment, a boy and a girl came down the street on their way to school, backpacks strapped shut with strips of leather. "Look!" they said in their language. "Money!" and each bent and picked up the coins and went on their way.

The young man smiled wanly at the proprietor, and the proprietor slammed the door.

Something changed that day. The rain never came, and passersby began actually greeting the young man—*Good morning*—children touched his sleeve, and the proprietor—whose business was merely normal—kept looking out and looking out. But that day, upon leaving, the proprietor's regular customers—usually mute, avoiding the young man's eyes—looked at him and greeted him with formal civility; it seemed to the young man that perhaps the proprietor had told them the story of the throwing of the money.

Very early the next day, the proprietor opened the door, stepped into the street, walked up to the young man, and put the requisite money into the his right hand. The young man lowered the sign, said *Thank you*, nodded his head, and went home.

I know this story is true, for I was that young man, and thirty years later I have returned to this city of that year of my youth, hair half-gone, my own belly like a balloon, standing at this moment at the dented zinc bar of that very café, the old proprietor bent now, leaning from a stool in the corner like a figure in a Daumier drawing, rising only when he needs to, slow in the body, slow in the eyes, a local student beside me telling me my own story, his version somewhat embellished. The story's grown in the years I've been gone—I was tall and handsome, he says—and he uses some words I quickly look up in my old tattered dictionary—*persistence* is one of them—and now he looks at the proprietor and makes that same native hissing sound and says, *He's like a man whose air has escaped him, and he can't get it back. And all the student wanted was an honest cup of coffee.*

Man of New Skin

A MAN OF GRANITE was composing a letter to a friend and paused a moment, staring, seeking just the right word, and found it, chiseled it, and when he looked down again he was inside a room in a third-floor city apartment, and he was covered with skin. It was all over him: his toes were skin, his feet, all the way up his belly and chest, arms, hands, head, everywhere.

For a minute he was afraid: he'd heard of skin, heard it described, heard that when a certain word was carved something like this might happen, but he certainly didn't know the word, and anyway this was an old Sedimentarian legend, and he was an Ignean, didn't believe it. His life so far had been no fairy story, that's for sure.

The man put his chisel down. He touched his left arm with his right hand. Smooth! Gliding right over it! And this hand, he thought—look how it can bend! The fingers flex! And the color so pretty—a kind of tan like sand, not at all like me.

He stood up, went to the big mirror. He shimmied a little, and his skin shimmied, too. He chuckled. Then he touched his body ever so slowly, from top to toe. This feels so *good*, he thought, and remembered how hard he'd had to knock his chest to get any feeling at all when he was stone.

Then he was afraid that if he'd turned to skin so quickly, he might just as quickly turn back to stone.

I'd better learn what it's like to have skin while I have it, he thought, and he hurried to the window and looked out. Everything looked different. He saw two blue signs below; they both started with the word *Rue*. They must be street signs, he figured, but in the land of stone, streets like that were called *Fissure*.

But he was only confused for a moment. It was attractive out there—trees and a wide, flat place to walk and other skin-people walking in the way that his body could move now, so much more quickly, more quietly than in the land of stone.

But down there, they had most of their skin covered with something, only their heads and hands not covered. Odd thing, he thought: have skin, cover it.

He saw that the sun was shining and wanted to feel its heat—he loved that when he was granite—and he bounded down the stairs—soundlessly, it seemed to him, and out into the street, where he joined the skin-people walking.

In sun, he could see tiny hairs, very thin, all over his skin, and when he walked he felt the wind buffeting his ears, breaking around his face. It was thrilling. He couldn't stop smiling. As he walked he loved the feeling of the rounded stones under his feet. One would get under his toes, then another under his heel. He liked that feeling very much, for stone hardly feels stone where he came from.

"Isn't this exciting?" he said to a man he was passing, but the man looked away.

He came to a crowded street now, giggling as his feet felt the grates of a subway, as its blast of hot air blew his hair, laughing as he turned a corner and found another wind.

He looked down at his body and saw that his penis was bouncing up and down as he walked—that never happened in stone—and he thought it funny, and again began laughing, walking faster to watch it jiggle faster, and he just had to share his joy with somebody, so he looked over to his fellow wind-walkers and said, "My penis is jiggling!" But for some reason they stopped walking, none of them joining in his laughter—a few, though, smiling, turning, continuing on their way. What a grouchy place, he thought.

When he got to the corner, two kind men wearing cloth of the same color blue talked to him. He was grateful for conversation. "We have to take you somewhere, sir—please come with us."

One man took his arm and led him to a car. "Your hand feels so *good* on my arm," said the man of new skin, but to his disappointment, the man in blue cloth let go.

What happened then was confusing. He was in a new place where kind people wore white cloth instead of blue, and he had the sense that he'd better not talk too much, because in their kindness people might want to talk in return, and all he really wanted was to get back into that sun, that wind.

They put him on a table and touched him in many places, and he liked that and said, "No, of course that doesn't hurt, it feels *great*," and they asked him many *why*'s, and he kept saying, "I just wanted to feel the sun and wind on my skin," and they said he had no "record," that he was not considered "dangerous" (*dangerous* was an important word in the land of stone; *record* he'd never heard), and they gave him some cloth, helped him put it on, told him he had to keep wearing it, and let him go.

"We don't want to see you here again," they said as he left, and he wondered why they'd suddenly become so unfriendly. Even in the land of stone, it was traditional to say, "Drop by any time" to a person leaving.

On the way home it began to rain: a warm, almost invisible rain that at first only wet his face, and he felt the rain must be a kind of gift; the hairs on his head dripped, droplets of water wet his face, found their way into his mouth. Then it rained harder, and he saw that his fellow walkers shielded themselves from the rain: strange domes of colored cloth bursting upward everywhere.

He was agitated—felt outside their world.

If I only took off my top cloth I could feel the rain on my chest, he thought, and did so, and people didn't stop this time—they looked at him and looked away, and that was okay with the man, and soon the drops were coming too fast to count, but they were counted somewhere by his skin, he was sure, as if a reservoir of happiness was being filled.

When he got home, the man of new skin stood in front of a mirror and looked. Beads of water all over his body, all over his face. He felt he'd been to a feast where no one but he was eating. He was tired and went to bed.

The next day was bright, and hot, and he walked, fully covered with cloth, feeling great to be alive and in skin, but somehow deprived.

He loved touching his own skin so much that he wanted to see what other skin felt like, so at a stoplight he saw a man with big naked arms and went up to him and put both hands around the big part of the man's arms and said, "Nice skin!"

"Thanks," the man said. "Want to come up to my place?"

"Oh, no," said the man of new skin, "I just wanted to touch your arm."

At another stoplight, there was a woman with a long wrap of cloth that started at the very top of her legs; even in cloth, he liked the round shape of her from behind, and he was sure she wouldn't mind if he stood next to her and just ran his hand down that shape to learn about the skin in there. So he did, and she gave him a most unpleasant look, and stepped away from him, and when the light turned green she strode quickly away. Though he was hurt by her unfriendliness, still, he thought, this is a better day than yesterday. That day had started out fun but got confusing.

He came to a man sitting on the walkway and holding out his hand. The man had a huge nose, and the man of new skin touched the man's nose, and the sitting man didn't seem to mind at all. It was like stone, really—pocked and chipped and blue-veined—but warm, and the man of new skin liked the way the tips of his fingers could know the difference between the *in* of those pores and the *out*.

As he walked on he noticed that he liked to watch the women's breasts. Some moved in quick circles as the women walked, circles independent of one another, and it appeared that some breasts under their cloths were harder, some softer.

This was never true in the land of stone. All the women's breasts were hard in the land of stone, and when women walked not much really moved, especially in the Igneans. Every once in a while some Sedimentarians came into town, and if you looked very closely, you could notice a shift in their parts as they moved. Even in the land of stone the man liked this very much, but here in the land of skin it was glorious.

So in the middle of the walkway, the man saw a woman coming toward him, and he said, "Stop, please," and put his left hand on her left breast and said, "Thank you, that was instructive, that felt very nice."

But this was not at all the same as when he felt the man's arm at the corner. The woman hit the man of new skin very hard on his face. The whole side of his face felt hot.

"That certainly wasn't called for," said the man of new skin, but there was shouting all around and again men in blue cloth came, different men this time, these not as kind, and they took his arm roughly and led him away.

For days, then, everything was confusing. They put him in a room made of square stones, people came and talked to him about what he did, put him on "trial," said cruel things about him, and put him in another stone room alone for thirty days.

At last he was freed: delighted again to be walking in wind, headed home.

But again, things got confusing. As he passed a corner near his home a pretty woman wrapped in a very short cloth was leaning against a building. She asked him something— something he had to ask her to repeat, something that seemed to be about an offer of employment in the service of wind. Seeing that she was not like the other women on the street—so unfriendly in this warm land of skin—he of course said yes, he'd like that very much, that he was ready to be employed.

"No," she said. "Not here. Come up to my room in that hotel over there." And so they went to the room and the woman showed that indeed she was a woman of skin, and without at all referring to the promised employment she touched his body in many ways until he felt confused, cloud-like, until he felt that he was snowing onto his own stone, as if he himself were the first snow of the new year in his old world.

"Stay with me," he said, but she stood and put on her cloth and asked for money.

"I didn't know you wanted money," he said, "I'm unprepared. Perhaps I'll have it after that employment you spoke about," he said.

Soon there was a man in the room with big arms like the man on the corner, but nowhere near as friendly. The man struck him, right there on the bed—did not even allow him to stand, to ask the questions he still had.

There is no pain like that of a man of stone who has become a man of skin and is beaten, and he wept deeply, not knowing how to defend himself against the blows, their increase.

These people, too, sent him home.

When he got home, all his skin pulsed with pain, and he turned on the light and saw himself in the mirror. Many new colors, stone-like colors, but much red, too.

He wanted to go stone again, to go granite, to be with his hard-fired, consistent people.

But all his brittle wishes did nothing. He went to the window and looked at the pavement in envy. There was nothing he could do. He did not know the cause of his leaving the land of stone, and he could not cause himself to go back. He stayed in the land of skin.

He is among us. I know him. And I can tell you that every once in a while, late at night, the man of new skin climbs to the roof of his building, strips off his cloth, and stands in the rain. Then he puts on the cloth again and goes back in.

The Choreographer

At last, he understood that all his life had been chore-
ography for his funeral. He came to this not through therapy,
but during a walk in the woods on his friend Bernstein's
sheep farm in southern Oregon.

It was January, he'd been invited to spend the week, and
early Monday before the others were up he went walking
in the cold, the maples still holding brilliant leaves on their
lowest branches, his boots crunching ice along the path. He
stopped at the pond, broke off a pane of ice from its surface,
held it up, saw his own crazed reflection there, an abstraction
he was proud to appreciate, and he wanted to tell Bernstein
about it, Bernstein a painter, tell him about the fascinating
distortion, the outline of the nose limning a raised ridge in
the ice, the chin line carved along the edge—he wanted his
friend to know that he understood abstraction. And when
he came back into the house, went into his paneled room
overlooking the sheep pen, took off his jacket and gloves and
rehearsed his quick speech about the glassy ice, he knew then,
in the quiet of the house, that the entire speech was meant to

plant in Bernstein's head the possibility, the suggestion, of his painter friend rising at his funeral and saying, "I just want to say that he understood abstraction."

He sat on the bed, and in a moment less of honesty than of a long life's filtration, saw that almost everything he had said or done in his life after, say, age thirty, had been funeral choreography.

For decades now, he admitted, he'd pictured the exact room of his memorial: warm yellow light, metal chairs, a bank of windows revealing a mature garden, wine and hors d'oeuvres on a table at the rear, a crowd larger than the capacity of the place. A winter afternoon—perhaps not unlike what today's afternoon will be, he thought.

How familiar he was with that place. It had been his, detail after detail added, for thirty years now—was always there when he spoke, didn't speak, acted, didn't act.

When he was a lover, he was a lover in order that the beautiful woman he was caressing might, at that memorial, stand—only at the end, mind you—and in a soft voice say *I just wanted to mention that he was a wonderful lover*, and then ten women, emboldened, would stand and in a quickly accelerating crescendo say *He certainly was*, and it would be a moment of great humor, memorable.

When he took time to speak with the postman who brought his mail and he asked after the postman's kids, it was in hope, really, that the postman would rise that same day and say *He always asked about my family, always remembered my kids' names.*

When he was a teacher, he taught not so much to share knowledge but to assemble a legion of potential memorial-goers, each of them standing to say *He taught me so much*, and *He was so important to me formatively*, and *The world will never be the same*. . .

And so it went: when he visited the sick, helped a neighbor change a transmission, bought season tickets to the symphony, studied the Ramayana, traveled to difficult places—all was toward memorial accolade: *He brought tenderness to everything he did. He'd give you the shirt off his back. He was an underground scholar. He knew more about John Cage than most musicians I know. He could name the streets of Nairobi in his sleep*, and of course, his friend Bernstein's abstraction comment, and his good wife positioned at the side of the room surrounded north, south, east, west by his four kids, all of them laughing and weeping.

He couldn't know, though, on this clear winter day in southern Oregon, that his memorial would be nothing like that.

His wife would have arranged a simple service in the Presbyterian Church, word of his death would not have gone out widely—one of his sons having missed the deadline for the obituary—and there was a storm: brutal rain, dangerous driving. Family and extended family would come, but Bernstein would be in Hawaii, the postman long dead, students spread around the globe, most of them hearing of his death only months later, and no lovers: not one. Why would they have heard? A neighbor would rise to say *He helped me change my transmission, and I still have the scars to prove it,* but the little joke would have gone over badly, sounding strangely bitter.

But for this Monday morning, he was at peace with himself, the confidence of a choreographer just before opening night, certain that his dancers know their moves, that the stage is clean, the music cued, the lights just right, the understudies stretching in the wings.

Notes on the Music

Much of the music referred to in these poems is easily accessible. Should the reader be interested, here are particular versions:

PAGE 19: "The Tones of Koto"
"Hachidan," from *Nanae Yoshimura: The Art of the Koto, Volume 2* (Celestial Harmonies, 2002).

PAGE 39: "Sephardic Airs"
Aires de Sefarad: 46 Spanish Songs for Violin and Guitar, Jorge Liderman/Duo 46, Matt Gould, guitar, Beth Ilana Schneider, violin (Albany Records, 2006).

PAGE 63: "Pasencore"
In service of the narrative, the author has invented the titles of songs mentioned in this piece. But versions of particular songs did engender them:

For the Bach song: Cantata BMV 204 "Ich bin in mir vergnügt," Aria "Die Schätzbarkeit der weiten Erde," from *J. S. Bach: Arias for Soprano and Violin*, Kathleen Battle and Itzhak Perlman (Deutsche Grammophon, 1992).

For the Schumann: Frauenliebe und-leben Op. 42, "Nun hast du mir den ersten Schmerz getan," from *Schumann: Frauenliebe und-leben, Brahms: 8 Songs*, Lorraine Hunt Lieberson and Julius Drake (Wigmore Hall Live, 2008).

For the Brahms: Lieder Op. 43, No. 2, "Die Mainacht," from *Johannes Brahms: Lieder*, Anne Sofie von Otter and Bengt Forsberg (Deutsche Grammophon, 1991).

For the Paolo Conte: the whole Conte gestalt. Conte is an Italian singer, composer, pianist, vibraphone player, visual artist, and lawyer whose voice and performance resemble an amalgam of Tom Waits,

Randy Newman, and Charles Bukowski. Recommended is *The Best of Paolo Conte* (Paradiso Communications, 2003).

PAGE 76: "THE EXTRAORDINARY ACCORDIONIST"
"L'indifférence," sometimes called "Indifférence": a wonderful old version, remastered, Tony Muréna playing, *Les Accordeons de France* (Arkadia Chansons, 1999).

"La Foule": The eminent Wynton Marsalis on trumpet and Richard Galliano on accordion, *From Billie Holiday to Edith Piaf: Live in Marciac* (Rampart Street/Jazz in Marciac, 2010). Also, as amazing as ever, the Edith Piaf version, *Edith Piaf 30th Anniversaire* (EMI France, 1994).

"Les Yeux Noires": Paucity of great renditions on accordion. Better to hear what can be done with this song by listening to Stochelo Rosenberg's astonishing guitar rendition: *Stochelo Rosenberg: Seresta* (Vintage Guitar Series, 1999).

PAGE 80: "GESTURE"
"Rain on Rahoon Falls Softly...": The title is from the first line of Joyce's "She Weeps for Rahoon," one of thirteen poems published in 1927 by Sylvia Beach at Shakespeare and Company in Paris. The volume was called *Pomes Penyeach*, and sold for one shilling (twelve pennies), or twelve francs. The poem was written in Trieste in 1913 after a visit to the Rahoon grave of Michael Bodkin, the young love of Nora Barnacle and model for Joyce's character Michael Furey, the singer whose memory Gretta Conroy evokes in the final passages of "The Dead." The composer Muriel Herbert, a friend of Joyce, wrote a version whose melody Joyce claimed was better than his words. The soprano Allish Tynan sings it in a recording of Herbert's songs (*Songs of Muriel Herbert*, Linn Records, 2009).